The Lost Poem

English Language
The Lost Poem
(Poems)
 by
Ismail Meladi

Published in November 2023
by Decan Imprint Publishing Co.
Reg. Off: Sharjah Publishing City
Free Zone Sharjah, UAE.
Phone: 00971-551830334
Email : decanimprint@gmail.com

Cover Design :Lemonello
Printed at
Manipal Technologies Ltd

06/23-24/Sl.No.06/125/230gsm Artpaper
ISBN 978-93-5973-816-1

The Lost Poem

(Poems)

Ismail Meladi

Decan Imprint

Ismail Meladi

Ismail Meladi was born on 20th April 1962 at Meladi, Payyoli in Calicut District of Kerala in India. He started his journalism career as the first Delhi Reporter of Madhyamam Daily in 1987. He was the Delhi Bureau Chief of Mangalam Daily until 1997, when he left for the UAE to join the Gulf Today Daily as a Senior Reporter/ Chief Sub-Editor. Ismail joined Dubai Municipality's Media Section in 2002 as Senior Media Officer. After a brief stint of five years as Media Relations Officer with RasGas Company Limited, Qatar, Ismail returned to his old place, Dubai Municipality Media Section in August 2016 to look after the Media Relations and retired from there mid-2023.

Ismail has been publishing poems since 1986. He has received many laurels including the Haritham T V Kochubava Award for poetry (2023), Palm Aksharamudra Award (2019), Arabia Aksharasree Award for Literary Achievements (2005) and SahrudayaPadiyath Award for Poetry (2007).

His published books in Malayalam include "Dilli" (Delhi), "Chintheritta Kaalam" (Chiseled Time), "Indraprasthathile Atheedriyangal" (The extra-sensory experiences in Delhi) and "Vaarthakal Ormikkaanullathalla" (News is not to be remembered). In addition to that Ismail has published a collection of poems in English called "The Migrant Sandstones," which was also translated into Tamil in the name, "PulamPeyar Manal Thukalkal."

Ismail's poems were published on www.poetry.comand many anthologies, including "Timeless Mysteries," published by International Library of Poetry, Maryland, USA. He has translated three book sand many poems from Malayalam to English and stories from English to Malayalam. Ismail became the first Indian to present his poems in Arabic at the Emirates Writers' Union in 2010. He has published numerous poems and articles in Malayalam, English, Arabic, Hindi, Tamil and Persian. Ismail is also credited with translating UAE Arab poets, Shihab Ghanem, Ibrahim Al Hashimi, Ibrahim Mohammed Ibrahim, Salha Ghabish, Hamda Al Murr Al Muheiry, Humaid Al Darea and Abdulla Bin Qusair and stories of Aisha Abdulla Mohammed Ali from Arabic to Malayalam. He has also worked as director, script writer, narrator and presenter for many TV programmes in Malayalam, English and Hindi.

Email: ismail.meladi@gmail.com

Friends' Foreword

A foreword should be written by someone who knows me, my concept of life and more importantly, my poems and style of writing. So, I requested my close friends from the writing fraternity to pen a few lines about my poetry.

Sufi who reached Dubai from Meladi via Delhi

Ismail Meladi, whom I fondly call Ikkakka, has been a strong presence in the literary world for the last four decades. He started his literary career through journalism by writing articles and poetry collections. The first collection was named after the country's capital, Delhi, which was his initial centre of activity. Recently, he wrote "Indraprasthathile Atheendriyangal," a collection of his Delhi memories. "Chinteritta Kaalam" or Chiselled Time was another beautiful poetic dedication in which he depicted the pulse and progress of expatriate life like a picture on the canvas. A multi-lingual personality, Meladi's poems have been translated into many languages. This is the second book in English and the first was "The Migrant Sandstones." Meladi's poems are not mere rhetoric or written for timepass. They precisely mark the politics, the society's concerns and anxieties.

Some examples from his earlier poems:

"...After that, the use and meaning of light changed sense was sent out of the light, and the light was outcast from the word." (The Lantern)

"…Their wishes were being sucked in by the chimneys of factories
Hopes are being driven far away along with the herds of cows."
(Indian Images)
"This world never sleeps for a moment
The people of this world do not wake up
even for a moment."
(Truth)
How simply an all time and universal bare reality has been scribbled in three or four lines. But it touches our hearts so deeply. We do not wake up even while seeing the injustices and violence that are happening day and night. At the same time the world that rains fire does not sleep also. This writer has the unique characteristics of keeping everyone close to his heart in any crisis and making them happy with his 'love and favours.'

Just as the "Trees hang down due to the arrival of fruits," the beauty of his character must be the richness of his knowledge and experiences.

Best wishes for the new book. Let this be read more than any other book.

Shaji Haneef (Poet, Short-story Writer and Cultural Activist)

Meladi's poems
training ground for young poets

Many self-proclaimed poets face dearth of proficiency in language. While there is freedom to write about anything, and opportunities are available to develop style and techniques, such writers, devoid of a strong vocabulary, etymology, and in-depth knowledge of the magic of language, should be careful. The in-depth poems of Ismail Meladi are a good school for them to practice. The structure of Ismail's poems is like a sculpture carved on the Rosewood without giving too much attention to detailed ornamentation. Fountains of ideas can be seen oozing out from every organ. In some, it might be cool and in many it is hot or very hot. You can see in it a journalist's open eyes. However, newspaper language does not hijack his poems.

It follows the internal and external movements of society and keeps a third eye on its forehead. Many emotional moments do not make the poet angry as they used to because of the repetition of scenes. A maturity of empiricism and sentimental interpretations has swept the hyper-romantic connotations from that language. But, for that reason, poetry does not become eulogies of transitory worlds. For Ismail Meladi, his writings are a seasonal dance of a cyclical journey from Payyoli to Delhi, from there to Dubai and back to his weaknesses of the cultural practices of Calicut. Here, this poet's attempt to find poetic senses, separate from prose, will be of great benefit to poetry lovers. Congratulations to those poems and to the poet, who keeps life on one hand and philosophy on the other.

P. Sivaprasad   (Poet, Orator)

Meladi's poems
address nuances of human conditions

To some people, writing is a way to address different echelons of the human condition. It is absolutely a part of political awareness. Often its traces are found in the poetry. But it is never an unexpected manifestation. In this sense, Ismail Meladi's poems address the nuances of the human conditions. When he talks about the various aspects of life around him through poems, it takes the reader to a new age. It has romance, expatriation, and protest against the evil aspects of the system. Thus, the poet Ismail Meladi records the times too through his writings.

EK Dinesan (Social commentator, Author)

Poems readable beyond time

Ismail Meladi has a penchant to carve out the sights seen in different contexts in different times into a poem, readable beyond time, which is quite admirable. The variety of topics he chooses lead readers to a different level of thought. Poems such as "Dislodged Voice, "Post-Consciousness" and "Dark Circle" stand out for their diversity of ideas.

The wealth of experience he acquired from his life journey and journalism adds to the brilliance of his poems. Ismail Meladi's writings are translated into different languages like Arabic, English, Hindi, Persian, Malayalam and Tamil and the readership increase is due to the acceptance of the writer's thoughts, attitude and writing style.

Let this poetry collection reach out to many people who love to read poems. Best wishes to my elder brother poet and his new poetry collection.

Preethi Ranjit (Short-story Writer, Cultural Activist)

Meladi's poemspenetrate readers' minds with the sharpness of a diamond needle

When the poems penetrate into the minds of the reader with the sharpness of a diamond needle, it remains indelible. I have felt that Ismail Meladi's poems are deeply rooted in his experiences. Perhaps the perspectives and intense experiences that are carved out of the topics he receives as a media person, helps him to use a variety of subjects for his poems. A writer is remembered only when his poems are capable of satisfying the minds of the readers. Ismail Meladi's poems definitely offer food for thought to the reader, which exactly is the reason for fetching more readers to his poems. As they are translated into different languages, his poems can surely find readers in many parts of the world. All the best for the new book.

Praveen Palakkeel   (Novelist, Cultural Enthusiast)

Beauty of Meladi's poetry increases each time one reads it

Gentle and loving in nature, Ismail Meladi's poems are deeply insightful. The beauty of his poetry increases each time one reads it and tastes its richness. His usage of the language is truly heart touching. The clarity of Ismail Meladi's mind and his views towards life is evident in his poems. His style of poetry moves the reader's minds. I hope and pray that he scripts many more poems that captivate his readers. In this regard, I am certain that Ismail Meladi, my elder brother, will never disappoint us.

Sajna Abdulla (Short-story Writer, Cultural Activist)

Meladi's poems are like an archer's bow

Ismail Meladi's poems are like an archer's bow. It hits the spot, creates an impression and leaves an irrevocable mark on the reader's minds. Ranging from sweet nothings about love to the harsh realities of the world, his poems tackle a wide variety of topics and leaves on wondering what he will write about next.

Nasreen Abdulla   (Journalist, Orator, Personal Trainer)

Contents:

Clouds that never pour down

The address becomes a shadow
and sets out in search of the addressee

The letter with love in possession
is in search of ink for writing

The words full of expression
seek lips to speak out

The song with all its rhythm
awaits an ear

The heart overflowing with love
begs for a lover

Stars with their shining light
knock at the sky's door

The clouds search incessantly
for a land to pour down.

Yield

We put the manure of jealousy
for the best yield

To get a hundred percentage harvest
we plant hatred

To bring out the best bunches of grains
we pluck out the unwanted growth of love

To increase productivity
we use hybrid politics

For the yellowness of grains
we mix the ashes of religion

For the fertility of the earth
we import foreign monopoly

For extra high profit
we include anger

For short-term gains
we will sacrifice anything,
including us, our generation,
even the vitality of this land.

News is not to be remembered

Ensnaring memories and dreams
and raping them again and again
the letters unleash a roar

Counting and gathering
even the scraps of consciousness,
knocking them down and tying them up
the group of news vanishes

Proliferation of the arrows of voices
 that repeatedly come and strike aimlessly
on the ears of a pierced life

Meanwhile, in which pile of information
should I search to dig out the self-lost man
and bathe him in innocence?

Jungle Episode

There are cultural check posts
forty times an hour
one should pay the loyalty tax
exposing the heart,many times,
no papers are accepted

Words should not tilt an inch to the left or right
they will provide the pot of history,
testification should be on level with that,
your word water should reflect their faces

You should drink 100 ml of condensed patriotism
every morning immediately after waking up,
or, beat up yourself and extract your juice

New word toys are no more allowed for playing
gather the old withered leaves and paint afresh
pack them in bags without being damaged a bit
untouchability distance between benches is a must

None needs to have own faces on ID cards
paint same color in all photos
modify them and wear on your chests

Bend and fold the world
as small as the eyeholes of the veil,
darkness shall enter without closing the eyes,
outside breeze would also take a diversion

Pluck out the plants from the roots,
this sun heat is not enough for them to grow,
let not this greenery washed away
drenched in this soft cold rain, isn't it!

Introversion of meanings

Meanings come back
as fast as they ran in

As soon as it rises,
without letting it shine at all,
the meaning sun becomes silent
in the captivity of clouds

The meaning children drenched in rain
sob desires in their fever beds

The meaning legs that wished to rock and roll
can't take a step due to the weight of the chains

The words that are not polished enough
crawl in the throat seeking the right rhythm

The meaning dexterity that doesn't go sky high
ends up in the swamp of fear on its way toabyss.

The Lantern

Let's kindle that lantern once again
Didn't we extinguish it,
after a long-standing effort.
Let's resist the cold wind
and the torrential rain
for it to burn as a slight but true light

It had burned feebly and sometimes clearly
on the banks of the paddy field
and danced along with the songs of the mud

It must be still burning,
though with little flickering
on the memories of the time in hiding

It gave company without fail
to all the evening discussions on the culvert,
it lit up high along with Sartre and Camus
on the way back until the compound wall,
it was part of the friend circle,
until the neon light encroached,
turning the night into day

After that,
the use and meaning of light changed,
sense was sent out of the light,
light was outcast from the word.

The feeble light it created
on the first floor of the shop,
had raised the mercury level
in the thermometer of fists,
the voice needle in the throats
had run faster than ever.

Later,
The fingers on the fists
started straightening before folding,
counted and confirmed repeatedly,
before folding the fists
the voice needle in the throats bent,
and sometimes it got broken too.

In the love moonlight of the alley,
it hummed the flowy lines of Ghazal,
sitting on the doorsteps of the front yard,
until the computer occupied the room upstairs

After that,
the love, treading past the moonlight,
vanished in the dark oblivions of the sky.

Even while trembling, it used to light up
the rutted wrinkled curves of the gray country road,
when the road colour was blackened with tar,
the gray rushed in the luxury BMW car,
forgetting to take the light along the journey.

The piece of peacock feather secretly kept
in the textbook of Grade 2,
its colours used to spread its wings
and dance in the light of the lantern,
increased by tightening the wick
when the flash blinked from the game CD
the Grade 2 textbook was abandoned
in the dusty storeroom on the rooftop.

Dream of an Olive leaf

Blood flows like a stream
from the branch of Olive
and from the den of memories
it overflows as a river of fight

[1]Kufiya becomes red
as the shine of youthfulness,
as the praising song of truth,
taking pride in enduring pain

There arises the cry
of multiple generations
as the sprouting grain of the land
and the color of the earth darkens

As the brides of death,
The torches of the land,
burn inside the people's hearts,
hopes rise as acclamatory shouts

The fangs of the chariot
stab causing pain
to the tender hearts
and breaks the buds of hopes

A thousand torches fly away
through the river of hearts
the bone of life crumbles

Truth spreads
like a perennial tongue,
untiring hands
and unwavering voice

The fire flares up
beyond the oceans
along with the minds,
and the ring stones crack

The cloud of kindness melts
in the valleys of skies
as the green of Olive leaves
and as the dream of grief

The boundary walls that rankle
as a wound in the heart of the land crack
and the child's steps stabilize

Do not throw again
manifold anxieties
to the mother's heart
that is already a fire pit

We are immersed in fun,
in intoxicated sleep,
without uttering a single word
and finally, dream of this Olive leaf burns out.

¹Kufiya: It is a chequered black and white scarf that is usually worn around the neck or head by Arabs and Palestinians

Post-consciousness

After the flood ended
they looked up in the sky
love clouds are about to rain
It was really bad not lifting the face
from the mobile phone for so long

When flood raised the water level
I saw outside my gate
a friend flows as a stream
his boat is full with
torn sacks of memories

While crying 'online'
without even talking to myself,
locked up in my room,
I heard the roaring sound outside,
words are descending through a rope
on the terrace of the neighboring house.

Circle of darkness

Do not fall for the firefly
passing beside you,
what if a tiny light cut into
the darkness of the head

Do not even wear
a plastic smile of your face,
what if a drop of honey
ooze out of your heart

Close your ears and lock them,
painting them with lead metal coating,
what if a letter gets in
through the wind

Name should become a fight, isn't it?
and the tongue a pain,
what is the fun
if the road is not blocked.

The lost poem

That was the poem I have taken away,
to be thrown out, it was when
the thoughts started running
towards all four sides, aimlessly

For her, it was just a piece of paper,
scribbled and damaged for nothing
For me, it was life that doesn't line up,
no matter how hard I draw.

Bull's eye

Bull's Eye, Malayali's favorite dish,
it's the conscience that spreads out

There is only a peripheral red,
one touch is enough, it will slide down
in many directions on a slippery mode
it will stick on any edge of the plate

However, a clearly white base
that cannot be chewed down easily
will remain at the end.

Everyone's favorite tune

I am dancing on my tune
you are running on your tune

There is never a common rhythm,
everyone's favorite tune

A new life music is
smoldering constantly

Outcries multiply with increased enthusiasm
they go wild parting ways to different directions

All the songs run away
from the pitch of life

Row after row, houses proliferate
no public road, only ways for fighting.

News from Kerala

How long has it been
since you put your hand
on a friend's shoulder, guys?
Have all my local 'friends'
left the place together?

How long has it been
since I looked without the blink of an eye
at a baby's milky smile, comrades?
Have all the babies forgotten to smile?

My dear people, I forgot village pathways,
mesmerized by the single straight view
as only the way home tangled in my mind
Is there a world outside my home?

It's not at all necessary to open my mouth
since I started talking with the fingers,
I am hesitant to lift my head
How do I smile?

Sloughing Kerala

There are many snakes in Kerala
that slough on a daily basis
You will get enough skin,
whenever necessary
If it is not adequate,
you can import them
When you get embarrassed
after continuous sloughing,
some people become experts
in sloughing the embarrassment
As the people are becoming snakes
by walking and running
Kerala has become a python
outrunning its own map
That python is so indifferent,
no matter how many times it is hit on its head
no matter how many times stabbed on its body.

Narrow doors

The doors of Malayalee community
have become really small
and the number of windows
have become more in number
Different winds are flowing
through those windows
each room has been dumped
with multi-colored dusts
the floor is not at all visible.
The compound walls
grow taller each day
the metamorphosis of gates
are unbelievably strange
The main mission of all these
seems to be obstructing the vision
The place of the buried trees
are replaced by foreign plants
whose names are unknown
Colour of the premises changes,
alien soil shines with new vigour
Cages proliferate inside and outside
With daily increase of islands inside
I wonder, when is it next time
a Malayali can see another closely.

The sweat constituency

This is the sweat constituency,
toiling barren life's constituency
that draws transient pictures
on the hot sandstones

The dream trading sky constituency
where one reached straight up,
without falling or slipping over
the whirlpool in the ocean

Where everything gets frozen halfway through,
where unfurling colours dazzle your eyes,
making them half-closed,
though sun sprinkles saffron,
beyond the endless horizon

The stone layers flake off the mind,
where black river continues to flow
Though the ageing body retires,
the overtoiled hands
remain a branch to lean on.

Trajectory

The bridge that swallows all the skies ahead
walks back to itself instead of going ahead

The words that never emerge from the mouth
are sowing seeds in the ears

The look that reaches nowhere
is fixed in the eyes itself

The hands, deprived of movement,
extend to the four directions of the mind.

The Cultural Sindoor

The mind that ran away from the book
descended on the street
The tied-up cow was dragged out of the cow-shed
and was positioned in the middle of the street
then, with the accompaniment of music,
people sat on the cow's back,
travelled around the city, blocked the traffic
the cow was taken around
all the streets it was hesitant to walk
then, it was tied around the bamboo stick
sprinkled red colour on the face of the street
and said, they have painted
the hairline of the street
with the *Cultural Sindoor*[2].

[2]*Sindoor: A vermillion mark on the hairline of married Indian women*

The woman who sits alone in the park

The sky of looks will pour down
on the woman, who sits alone in the park
as the moments ticked by
web of doubts will continue to be woven

Guessing she is for sale,
masturbating with eyes,
hiding and appearing, all around her,
from youngsters to old men
are eager to shoot their questions
as the arrows of their desires

She struggles herself, melting in tension,
wrapping herself with the shawl of shame
to hide her big breasts that will rise up again
when her mind roars like a sea
in the unending miseries of life

Now, in a different rhythm,
the sighs of anxiety
will create waves around
and that wicked waves will soak
her silent shore of tears

Even when she is fully drenched
in the unending rain of sorrows
the doubtful hawks
will still be hovering around.

The overlooked grass

Rejected love is like the grass
that buds in the desert
and withers away in the sun for none
Even when it falls down, exhausted,
dries up and burns and decomposes,
it will remain undigested
in the womb of the earth
Rejected love is not destined to die
it's just overlooked,
it will always remain a silent cry
in the inner core of the earth
sometimes, the wind of time may unearth it
as the phosphorus of memories
that day, it will flare up unprecedentedly.

The invisible flute

The unique land of the great flautist,
who created an immortal spring of love
with the magic of his enchanting tune
that flows through the reed pipe

The beautiful land where affection flowed like honey,
where the prowess of a lover who always created
a charming sweet garden of love,
overflowing with happiness in women's mind

Today, that flute developed and became just a bamboo stick,
forgetting the enthralling song of the flute,
it cries out the thunderous language of punishment
that lands on the heads of poor cowherds.

The smell of the soil

Let's search digging deep into the fossils
to find out and have a better understanding
whether there were any signs in the history,
whether there were the costumes of culture

Let's find happiness in cutting and slicing
each and every layer of the soil
let's cut and tear the documents
by wielding the scepter of power

Let's measure the smell of the minds
with the measuring scale of the axe
until the blood oozes out incessantly
until the veins split and scatter

Let's squeeze and split the roots
divide one into two
transplant without leaving them to stick
until they wither and turn to charcoal in summer

Let's roll the chariot wheels again
and drive out the names all along
let's crush the bones again,
break down all the teeth

Let's spread the cloud of darkness
under the Aryan sky
let's roll again
the zodiac wheel of dark invasion

The overly modified dreams
fall down, and
the roots hug deeper,
spreads, fighting together

All the lines become straight ones,
the family domination comes to an end,
the words split the oceans,
new deciding lines are created.

Silent prayer

The house, becoming a tree,
is rooted in me alone,
Life crumbles and falls apart
in the blood stream of the silence
that grows in the wood
Words, becoming leaves,
bloom, blossom, and shine,
still end up as holes in the mouth

The eyes, becoming blue waters of sorrow,
look for the salt of desires,
at a time when other people's lips
should sing the sweetest of music,
the country flows like a snail
without any sound,
wearing the mask of anxiety

Even the crystal fish of love
that shines in the eyes of fellow human beings
are hooked on the arrow of doubt
Life with spouse became sheltered life,
a silent prayer, and a journey diving into the soul
far away, in the unseen depth of memories,
the breath of the dear ones
immerses in the infinity

I am twisting a rope into myself,
thoughts intertwine, and mate with silence.

Epitome of goodness
on the needle tip

World is centered on the mind of the needle tip,
man's footsteps are on a constant journey,
 and unknowingly move towards far away.
The embellishments of alienation
create lonely islands of darkness,
even the fleeing hopes limp and faint.
Even though the whole body is in a binding vortex,
the epitomes of goodness are trying hard,
by untying their minds and guarding the fence,
before the last breath in front of helplessness.
Blowing hard the breath of life on the fence posts,
the touch of kindness drinks sweat themselves.
Longing to hug in the mind distantly those kindness.

The dislodged voice

When the girl's tongue is chopped up,
the nation bleeds to death

When the color of man fades
in the mirror of the land,
the corpse of politics rots

When poison is sprinkled in thoughts
the buds of children get scorched

When the darkness thickens
children take up the task
of building a tunnel
for sighting the moonlight.

Mortuary

This world is a morgue
full of unknown corpses
'God' became the greatest Samaritan,
 who took care of every corpse
that had been left unclaimed over a long time
All sang praises to 'God,' who buried
all the corpses with due respect
One day, 'God' also passed away, untimely
But the body of 'God' has also been lying
unattended in this morgue for many centuries,
without anyone to take care of it
ungrateful human beings
do not even look back in that direction.

Noise

"If you had made a little noise,
if you had cried a little louder..."
it's not a cinema dialogue,
it's the soliloquy of a mute society...
When manufacturers of darkness
keep stinging with poison
in the depth of children's minds,
when the wings of the mother
are being slashed and sold one by one,
there are many hands still not raised,
there are many unspoken throats,
many hearts with stopped beating.

Downward journey of meanings

Words that gasp for breath
breath that struggles for words
The needles of the clock
that ceased working
The life's dictionary with
a realigned word layout
The journey of words
that gets vaporized
through the 'pro'gress of gases
The ribs that are pulled out
with the sword edges of texts
The legs that are cut
out of the earth incessantly
The soil that are coming off
from the heel every second
Every dry patch of earth is
a breath that drinks melancholy
Every drop of sweat
that is drained out
is a sea of desires,
a water surface of
intense expectations
When prayers are sent out
to pilgrimage one by one
trapped in darkness
all meanings are towed away by chariots.

Cold news

The cold news items, lying
in the old newspaper pages,
are looking at me mocking,
or, are they sobbing
or shedding tears?

It was me who sobbed on that day,
when the news was published,
many people were there to cry with me
Oh! what a ruckus and uproar was then,
unending noisy debates on TV channels,
the teashops also witnessed heated arguments
the girl, who lost her life, was not a 'stranger'
she became 'sister' to many, 'kin' to some others
she was glorified as the 'memorial of rape story'
the lava current of candles
to declare solidarity with the victim…

Bullshit…

I was also there among those
held the flags in the procession,
thinking that it would be a shame
if I didn't join the flow, because,
I am a 'member of the public society'
in the forefront of the 'reaction brigade'

The news is now frozen in the mortuary,
ants have taken away all the letters
in the newspaper page, one by one
the ants travelled in different countries,
in the land and in the sea, even in the air
they became swollen
with the digested letters of the news
they have now metamorphosed as humans,
searching for the victim in the latest news.

Straight stream

When the straight streams get obliterated by a crack
that occurred in the snow layers at the summit

History will flow with a sensuous slink
through the narrow mind paths

By repeatedly smashing its head on the rocks
of the dark time and get amputated

By falling deep into the crater of hatred
waiting for light infinitely

As water springing from unknown corners
joined by umpteen number of streams

Becoming a huge current with inner strength
it will head towards the true sky

Countless creepers will come down on that day
pushing away the dark clouds

All the water threads will join together and intertwine
to create the pinnacle of cleaning currents

By imbibing new energy from the equator on that day,
sun's northern solstice on the crossroads of history

The glorified statues will crash down on that day
they will join the corpses floating in Ganga River
The completely worn-out teeth of consciousness
the rocks of ego will crash down one by one

Crawling till the borders of infinite truth
they will fall flat at the feet of the eternal ascetic

The incessant currents will start flowing in the straight streams
Through the smoothened paths after all thorns worn out of
them.

Rope bridge

When the journey stopped
at the interval of rush
putting the belly under chain,
life eloped with death
to unknown destination

Broken into umpteen pieces
after the anger flared up,
the heart built a rope to the sky
and climbed up to the dream

The whip that tried
to lash out from land to land
was set on fire by the wind flow

On the sandbank of the mind,
dream stretched out the blade of grass.

What name do we call love?

What name do we call this love?
The drop of honey
from the flower of thought
that has blossomed between us?

Is it the smile that has been budding
again and again on your lips
but, still hesitant to blossom yet?

Or the hundreds and hundreds of stories
that are asleep on your eyes
without being read yet?

Is it the fragrance of your heart
that can be inhaled to
the inner layer of my soul?

Or the magical waves
that makes a seductive journey
the words make through the looks?

Is it the eloquent poem
of silent alphabets
that I feel in my soul?

Or the touch without touching
when I touch you in my mind
from distance?

Grave of truth

When my voice
that has been crushed,
again and again,
refuses to recognise me,
my shadow overtakes me

Where shall I go now
in search of my own voice

My face
that has been scratched
several times and
torn into many things
by different measurements,
dived into many oceans,
surfaced and downed again,
climbed many mountains,
rolled down and stuck,
wandered and shaken

Now, it has become
like a paper, where letters
have been faded.

The two legs with cracked feet,
have set out on their journeys
in search of the truth,
each on its own chosen path

Unable to take
a single step forward,
they are stuck
at the same place,
trying to consume time,
in a futile effort
to bury the body of the truth.

Chiseled time

It's a time when time is chiseled,
the voice cannot stand on its own,
you only speak with a sophisticated voice
the carpenter, who lost hope, chisels
to polish the face of the mother
Even by using foreign varnish
and a splash of colours
it did not end up beautiful too
The things that pile up
in front of the chiseling carpenter
include a mask worn by someone
at some time in the past,
the walking stick used by someone,
a blood-stained sheath of a sword,
bookshelf covered by spider webs,
dilapidated tables that are about to crumble,
moldy desks, smelly pen covers,
ruined pens dried up with ink,
frozen fingers, broken minds,
and chewed up thoughts.

Please take the face of the mother
to the beauty parlour
Smear and polish her face
with the musk turmeric
and blood sandalwood

that came in new packages
As they were applied,
the veins on the mother's face
started swelling, reddening
and becoming transparent,
and inside the veins,
it's a strange blood flow
to the opposite direction
Without even crying a bit,
without leaving a single sigh,
without even making a feeble groan,
the mother silently closes her eyes...

The torn sky

You teared away my sky
there were many maps
in the sky of my dreams
you poured and changed
your own colours there
you spilled lot of red
in many places,
replaced green with black,
mixed some other colour in blue,
my sky still remains torn out
dreams are flying out piece by piece,
in the wind you have blown in
from different sides
you are creating new skies
made of thermocol,
creating a magical world
of new dreams
in dazzling lights with
enchanting colour mixes
Can your thermocol sky,
that fades out before too long,
replace my sky?
In my sky clouds were
on an incessant journey
the cloud threads used to
always weave new dreams for me,
sunlight painted new colours
In what are you going to create a new sky
for me to replace the thermocol sky?

When the wind catches
the palm fronds

When the wind catches the palm fronds
the desert calls me welcoming
like the charming back neck
of the beautiful Arab damsel
who takes steps of the ³Na'asha dance,
throwing down her long hair into the front

The yellowy bunches of date fruits
reflect blossomed desires

When the wind becomes stronger
the sand becomes wild
and performs a destructive dance,
plucking out the dreams
from the chest of the migrants,
it blows out the memories even

When the hot wind catches rhythm on *Khuboos
the word hills become standstill,
ants eat out of the gathered hopes

As the severity of the heat increases,
the revolution in the veins start leaking,
sweat catches up on the bald brain

The bug bites of uncertainty
on the dust covered stack of books,
the steel bed decays

Many ships end up stranding mid-sea,
neither this shore nor the other
and on the other shore of the memories,
expectations that leak every day
commit suicide climbing on the skeleton houses
that still hope to have a roof

*³Na'asha: An Arabic dance form in which girls sway their hair to both sides *Khuboos: Arabic bread*

Weed houses

The fields ripened,
measuring virtues.
Tampered and levelled
the ground is now
filled with hatred.
The bunches of grains
have been transformed
into weeds and
vultures have pecked
them and flown away
pooping on coconut leaves,
dropping ashes too,
drying and burning them.
The bunches of grains
have grown now
and became houses,
just houses and houses…

The baby boy's journey

The baby boy who was playing
on the courtyard, around the land,
inside and outside the home,
suddenly walked past the passage,
and finally crossing the gate,
he landed straight away in Disneyland.
His favourite swing made of local rope,
 on the Moovandan Mango tree,
at his home premises,
was still calling him back
but, by that time, the baby boy
had climbed on the wild swing ride.
The coconut shell was asking him,
"how many sand breads do you want baby,"
by that time, he was enjoying
and rolling over inside the roller coaster
By the time his nanny came running,
gasping for breath,
with a bowlfull of sweet cookies,
the baby boy was wiping his hands
with tissue paper
after eating KFC chicken fillet.

Dried letters

Letters are laid out
on the balcony, to be dried.
Old people used to say:
"The letters sharpened by fire
do not wither in the sun"
But, now, fire is busy,
scrambling on the corridor
to grab the chair
Fire is now missing
from the thesis too
It's already outcast
from the fists long back,
and extinguished from the flags,
colour has been faded too.
The withered letters
are gathered from the balcony,
sprinkled with water and iron pressed,
the wrinkles straightened,
and made ready to wear for the ceremony,
was rushed in the BMW four-wheel drive
But the wrinkles came back again
in the wind on the way.
The letters, gathered from the balcony again,
were pledged in the Asian Development Bank.

Future of past and present

When I close my eyes
I am in the past.
What a relaxation!
Whatever happened
in the past
looks like a dream,
isn't it?
When I open my eyes
I reach the present
Oh, how terrible it is!
Whatever is happening
is not at all digestible
When the inner eye is opened
I will end up in the future
It's really shocking!
Oh my God, I can't face it...
Whatever is waiting for me
is not at all comfortable
Moreover, nothing is in my control
Let the inner eye be kept closed
Omniscience about three tenses is dangerous.

Crumbling images

Meladi, my birth place,
the unbroken image,
etched in my mind,
hanging in a colourful canvas,
as an enthralling sculpture,
an enchanting beauty

Years have blown vehemently
on that village
Has it been straightened
or heightened or has it been curved?
Today, I do not know my village
I have no idea what is foaming inside that
and what is being perished on the roadside
Is it the friendship, equality or harmony?
What is falling off the branches?
Is it the gooseberry of my school days?
What fell off from my book?
Is it the peacock feather of my childhood?

Today, this village has an image
entangled with mystery and complexities,
images are crumbling down one by one,
Shapes, postures and voices change
No, this is not my village,
this is not my playground too
Lots of goals are kicked here,
nets increase without a goalkeeper

Today, even my dear ones also crumble down
and become sculptures made of plastic,
the charm dies down, awkwardness arises,
faces with pasted smiles increase,
the feeling of acquaintance withers away,
walking ceased and legs have become machines

The horse eyes' reddishness gets projected,
unknown people lash the whips
There is no villager here now,
no village rhythm too.
Now, which land I belong to?
To read the expression on my face,
not even a mirror remains here.

What is heart's role here

When I got down to the road,
heart also accompanied me
On the way, some commotion, fracas
heart started beating slightly louder,
but limbs pointed fingers at it,
threatened it and ordered
"Just keep your mouth shut,
it's none of your business here"
Legs started retreating,
half lowering the eyebrows, eyes ran back,
ears dived inside, hands pulled back,
and then scratched the head
Lips said to itself:
What does that matter to me?

The fire of words

On the crossroads of
the silent darkness of life
with a desperate frozen face,
but with a golden heart,
let me describe with grief
the sorrows of forsakenness,
all those stories of complaints
that are getting grinded in the inner core

Each burning particles of thoughts
are falling out lazily
on the abyss path of eyes,
flaring up as a ball of fire
they beat around as waves of sorrows,
intense love and lamentation of prayers

It affects the threads of my mind -
the weakness of waves
that smash their heads on the rocks,
the worries of water's sadness
to part with the sand,
the unending touch
of the water threads
on the leaves

Pages of heart are burning
for the sacrifice of the flower
that longed for the sun,

and the roaring pain
of the life's struggle,
the destructive dance of tragedies
that cuts life into pieces

The blood oozing ocean
of the love that never runs dry
in the calendar of memories
The look of the rainclouds
of the torrent of unspoken words
The soundless splash
of unending pain

This is the scene of the time
that disappears in the dark downpour
Is it a critical point of time,
or the body of the flower of a waste wood,
or the smoky darkness of mind,
where the camphor lights extinguished
the mind sky, where moon has set,
the stupid pregnancy of stars
on the sky canopy

The coffin of the soul is being lifted
in the phosphorous house of dreams
Now, it's an infinite solo journey,
no more cheer songs or rhythms needed,
the percussion can be abandoned on the way,
the colours will slip out of the hand
to die down on the roadside

But words are my kith and kin,
they are safe in the inexhaustible mine,

deep inside my inner soul
words are my life's rhythm
and the shining fire of my tongue,
no wind or any crooked breaths
can ever extinguish the fire of my life

As the strong thoughts
and the bright feelings,
words will always stay intact,
in any deep corner
of my blood oozing mind
Words will shine again and again
burning in the furnace of experiences
and live long defeating the seasons.

The skyward journey of love

Heart left the hut
and found a new dwelling place
in the cyber café

Love, ending its walk
on the banks of the paddy field,
is travelling to the sky
through the mouse on the table

Stopping all flirting and whispering,
new dry imaginary lines
are being drawn
in frozen silence
The letters of love
that was not written
down on papers
stray from the herd,
stay hanging half way through
in some corner of some sky.

The butterfly lives

Yesterday:
The hinterlands where we used to play
in the childhood days,
making small butterflies lift the pebbles,
the multi-streamed memories
of make shift play houses we built,
the butterfly buzzing friendly talks.

Now, eyes are burning with sunlight dreams,
the bicycles are resting in silence
after the long journeys on the village paths
down the gravel hills of heart.

The *Kutty and Kol fly in memories
Footsteps are heard like "Each drop a pitcher rain"

In my eyes tender mango is oozing out its stain
Gooseberry is roaring in the mind as thirst
Mother is rushing as the pain of salt

Today:
Today at the friends' gathering
at my classmate's flat
the old ink plant was broken,
its juice spread as blood
small letters struggled for life on the slate

A dead and dried butterfly,
framed inside a glass work,
was hanging on the wall in his house,
a heart-breaking sight
that nailed a thousand nails
into the wall of my heart.

*Kutty and Kol (boy and cane) is a traditional game enjoyed by children
on a regular basis and not just during Onam in Kerala. A Kol is a stick
of wood about one cubit long (18 inches) and a Kutty is a small stick of
two-and-a-half inches long.*

Exercises of light

Light has no permanent place,
it can come and go anywhere
if needed, it can play hide and seek,
it can stay away, it can refuse to come

Full light, less light,
bright light, dim light,
reduced light, increased light,
light that is never switched off,
light that keeps on getting extinguished
There are many types of lights like these,
available in many patterns
It's up to you to decide
You can bask in the light available to you,
you can also adjust staying on the side
of the light lit by some other person
You may also pay money and arrange a light
and keep it on for you to be in the limelight
All will see you and congratulate you
until the light finishes,
after it gets extinguished,
it is impossible to say for sure
what will happen if the light goes out
Now, there is another possibility
you can light yourself up
and spread light for others,
only if you have the energy
inside you for that.

Salvation

Mankind escaped eternity
because the whole world
seemed to Eve to be a fruit.

Assimilation

This rain is pouring down
in my heart
I am far away

This river is overflowing
through my life
I am near

This thunder strikes
inside my head
Whether I am near or far.

Mirror

Delhi is a mirror,
any Indian can view
his face on that

Now, the mirror is faded
and blackened
Still, no one is daring
to clean the mirror,
black dust will spread
on to the hands and body
of anyone who does it.

After that,
no one will recognise him
Or, people will brand
black mark on him
If that happens,
no holy river could come
to his rescue.

Truth

This world never sleeps
for a moment

The people of this world
do not wake upeven for a moment.

Pain

Pain flows down
from the shoulder,
digging a canal
it reaches the wrist,
fingers, knees, feet
and finally,
the all-bearing earth,
absorbs the pain.

Understanding

It is when a bunch of miseries slid down
from the trousers of life,
he felt like laughing his heart out

It is when the tear drops of difficulties
started flowing as a stream out of her eyes,
he understood that life is so easy.

Realization

You should recognize
my every expression of love
It is the lack of recognition
that leads to big disasters
Unrecognized borders,
documents, strategies, voices,
even a sigh can become
the beginning of collapse.

Words

The words that pour down
again, and again
the words that are sung
as prayer offerings
the words that are spoken
densely sweet
the words that are stored
as wise old proverbs
the words that are shining
as holy utterings
the words that are gnashed
as false promises
the words that are lit up
as ghee lamps
the words that are licked
as honey talks
the words that are glittering
as full moon
the words that are burnt
as the ensemble of light
the words that are still flowing
as unending currents.

Life cooking

When people who received
a life that is not fit at all
are standing perplexed,
there are some other people,
not knowing how to prepare their life,
are cooking,
without peeling the skin,
and cutting into small pieces,
or even without washing,
they are using whatever they got
and place them all in the pot as it is
and add spices without any measurement,
the life cooked like this has an annoying smell
and has a bad taste that the tongue cannot approach.

It's prohibited

Do not tell
everything
to your wife
Do not ask
everything
to your children
Do not react
to everything
you see around
Do not show kindness
to anyone
without calculating
Do not help everyone
without looking
who they are
Do not spend time
at any place
for long
Do not smile
at everyone
open heartedly.

Separated people

All names migrated to the sky
and the addresses followed them,
humans became lonely on earth.

Policy declaration

My wife, who chopped my thoughts
and cooked them with curry

The children, who have broken and folded
my concepts and stuffed in my pocket

My neighbours, who cut the rope of my imagination
and tied a cloth line with that

My villagers, who pulled the bridge
and threw my desires into the river

Let me not declare my policy among these people
and swallow them.

I am on my planet

When a globe is spinning
inside my head
how can I not circle the sun,
In which planet am I
I am seeking an empty realm
in this universe,
nobody would have
prepared it for me
I should create
my own empty realm,
a silent void
without vibrations
A dark void
without noises of light
Let me build my planet
in blinding paces
and dense silences
Now, I am in my own planet,
I don't have satellites
My nerves of feelings
are wandering tired
in the infinite sky
Please leave me alone
in my own planet.

Viaticum

Oh, my baby,
I had put on your shoulders,
the weight of letters,
when you were just four
Later, it became
an unending burden,
it spread all over your body
When you struggled
in the heavy flow
of life's chemistry and maths,
I used to deliver sermons
 from the shore
Somehow you learned
the language of swimming,
you caught hold of
the wood of determination
in the voice deviation
of the water current
Even when you got to the shore
in one of the curves of the current
 I am still biding time helplessly,
by blessing and advising you
Oh, baby, your path
is determined by your feet.